FROM BELLY TO BABY

FROM BELLY TO BABY

a journal for pregnancy & baby's first year

LUCY RILES

Illustrations by Alyssa Nassner

ROCKRIDGE PRESS

Interior and Cover Designer: Jami Spittler
Art Producer: Sue Bischofberger
Editor: Vanessa Ta
Production Manager: Riley Hoffman
Production Editor: Melissa Edeburn
Illustrations © 2019 Alyssa Nassner
Author photo courtesy of © Kathy Schuh Photography

ISBN: Print 978-1-64152-616-6

This book is dedicated to my children:
Barbara, Tommy, Scotland, and Katie.
It is an honor to be your mom.
I love you more.

CONTENTS

INTRODUCTION

Congratulations on your pregnancy! Even before you knew you were pregnant, your body began nurturing the new life inside you, and as that new life grows, your body is adjusting in amazing ways to ensure your baby's well-being. No wonder this miraculous time is also exhausting.

Right now, it may feel like an eternity away, but that life you have created will shortly be nestled in your arms. The span of your pregnancy is but a small fraction of your entire life span. If you live to be 100 years old, this incredibly significant period will take only 280 days of the 36,500 days of your life. The morning sickness, swollen ankles, and other discomforts may feel endless, but they are all temporary. What is not temporary is the unconditional love and lifelong bond between you and your child.

Whether this is your first child or your fifth, your first girl or your first boy, this is a truly special time that only you and your baby share. So, it's only natural that you would want to document all of the precious moments.

My hope is that this journal for your pregnancy and your baby's first year helps you celebrate the momentous journey of motherhood. By providing week-by-week prompts, this journal allows you to record all the big milestones, from the first time you heard the heartbeat and felt the baby kick, to your baby's first words, steps, and birthday. *From Belly to Baby* also acts as a priceless keepsake in which you can express your hopes, fears, and dreams. Decades from now, you can gift this treasured journal to your child. When your child asks questions about his or her time of birth and measurements, you'll have *From Belly to Baby* to help remind you.

I hope this journal will also remind you that you are absolutely amazing.

(baby's name/nickname)

due

our *Family*

Parent:

About me:

Your grandparents:

About your grandparents:

Your aunt(s) and uncle(s):

About your aunt(s) and uncle(s):

Parent:

About me:

Your grandparents:

About your grandparents:

Your aunt(s) and uncle(s):

About your aunt(s) and uncle(s):

Your sibling(s):

_____

_____

_____

_____

About your sibling(s):

_____

_____

_____

Our story:

_____

_____

_____

_____

_____

_____

_____

_____

_____

Place family photo here

expecting
You

I first thought I could be pregnant when ....

I confirmed I was pregnant by ....

You were [planned / a surprise].

My first pregnancy symptoms were

The things I did to help alleviate pregnancy symptoms were

The first person I told I was pregnant was

I announced the pregnancy to family and friends by

Some memorable reactions from family and friends

included ....

....

....

....

....

....

....

....

....

My doctor: ....

My estimated due date is ....

If I had to guess, I think you are a [boy / girl].

If I had to name you right now, I would name you ....

....

> *A baby is something you carry inside you for nine months, in your arms for three years and in your heart till the day you die.*
>
> —MARY MASON

first
Trimester

Congratulations—you are going to be a mom! Ready or not, your baby is coming! You have approximately 40 weeks to prepare for your little one's arrival. Regardless, you may feel as if that's too little time to wrap your head around the idea of being responsible for another life, and that's okay. All you need to do is love your child unconditionally and do your best. Motherhood is not a job to master. Rather, it's a position in which you'll continually grow and learn.

The first trimester is not usually any mom's favorite time of pregnancy, but it is definitely one of the most amazing. Before the end of this trimester, all of your baby's major organs will become fully formed, and his or her bones and joints will begin developing with the support of nutrients and oxygen provided by your placenta.

Creating and growing another human is both miraculous and exhausting, so don't be surprised if you feel fatigued and nauseous during this trimester. It is completely normal and common to experience morning sickness, which is caused by an increase of hormones in your body. But don't be fooled by the term "morning sickness," because you may experience symptoms morning, noon, and night.

Hands down one of the most exciting experiences of the first trimester is when you hear your baby's heartbeat for the first time. Between weeks 8 and 10, you will go in for your prenatal visit, during which your doctor will be able to detect your baby's heartbeat using a fetal Doppler. Consider bringing a loved one with you to share in this monumental moment. The thrill of hearing that heartbeat can make up for the not-so-pleasant symptoms of morning sickness.

Week 8

Baby is the size of a blueberry

measuring about 0.5 inch. Heart and eyes are fully formed. Lungs, hands, and feet begin to form.

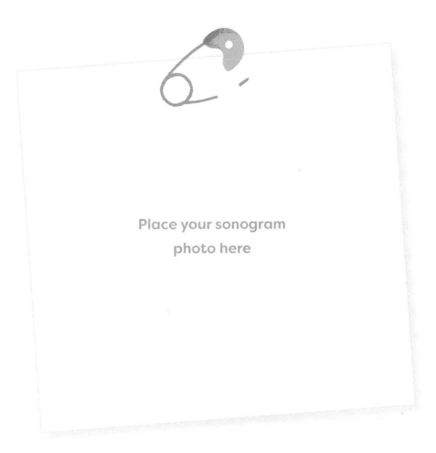

Place your sonogram
photo here

Your doctor can now officially confirm what those home pregnancy tests have been telling you for weeks: You are going to be a mom! Your first prenatal visit should take place sometime between weeks 8 and 10. This visit provides an opportunity to ask your doctor about all the dos and don'ts of pregnancy. There are no dumb questions when it comes to your health and the health of your baby, so ask away.

I first thought I was pregnant when

When I found out, I

I told .... first
by [how did you share the news?]

I am due

My reactions when I saw saw you on the sonogram:

I believe the choice to become a mother is the choice to become one of the greatest spiritual teachers there is.
—OPRAH

Baby is the size of a strawberry

measuring about 0.75 inch. Major organs are now in place. So are all major joints, which can now move and groove.

Just as the excitement of sharing your pregnancy news begins to settle in, symptoms of morning sickness may appear. Morning sickness, which is triggered by an increase of hormones in your body, can include exhaustion, dizziness, vomiting, and sensitivity to smell. These symptoms are very common and are a promising sign that your placenta is developing properly. Another upside of morning sickness is that your hair may be becoming lusciously thick.

So far, I'm experiencing [morning sickness, early pregnancy symptoms, etc.]

The scents I'm sensitive to are

The foods I'm craving are

The foods I don't want to eat anymore are

Whether your pregnancy was meticulously planned, medically coaxed, or happened by surprise, one thing is certain—your life will never be the same.
—CATHERINE JONES

Baby is the size of a prune

measuring about 1.25 inches and weighing around 0.25 ounce. Hair, fingernails, and bones are developing. Fingers and toes are starting to separate, and all the vital organs are now starting to grow at a rapid pace.

During your next prenatal visit, which usually takes place around week 10, your baby's heartbeat might be detectable with the help of an ultrasound transducer called a fetal Doppler or, more likely, with a regular ultrasound, so invite a loved one to join you. The moment you hear your baby's heartbeat, your own heart will skip a beat.

I first heard your heartbeat

My first reaction was

I think you might be a [boy / girl] because

Names I'm considering:

Children are the wisdom of the nation.
—AFRICAN PROVERB

Baby is the size of a lime

measuring 2 inches in length. Baby is now kicking, stretching, swallowing, and yawning. The nose and mouth have become more defined, and tooth buds are beginning to appear under the gums. At this point, your placenta has also started to provide your baby with essential nutrients and oxygen.

Although the symptoms of morning sickness should soon be subsiding, your pregnancy hormones are just getting started. Don't be surprised if one minute you find yourself complaining to a grocery store manager because the store stopped selling your favorite brand of hot sauce, and the next minute you are ugly crying in your home just from watching an insurance commercial on TV. This is totally normal. Blame the pregnancy hormones. And remember, only 200 more days to go!

My favorite thing about being pregnant so far is

My least favorite thing about being pregnant so far is

As a mom, I hope to be

My hopes and dreams for you:

I feel more beautiful than I've ever felt because I've given birth. I have never felt so connected, never felt like I had such a purpose on this earth.
—BEYONCÉ

Baby is the size of a plum

measuring 2.5 inches in length and weighing 0.5 ounce. Major organs are fully formed, and the kidneys are beginning to produce and excrete urine. Your first ultrasound or Doppler ultrasound scan allows you to finally see your precious little bundle.

Your uterus is now the size of a grapefruit. Before pregnancy, it was the size of a pear. You are now in the final stretch of the first trimester and likely at the tail end of morning sickness. Your appetite and newfound energy should begin to replace nausea and fatigue. Carve out some time for yourself. Plan a relaxing trip or find a nearby spa. You may not have much time for rest and relaxation after the baby arrives, so pamper yourself while you can.

What I'll remember most about the first trimester:

When I first saw you on the ultrasound, I felt

How I shared the pregnancy news with family and friends:

Before you were born, I carried you under my heart. From the moment you arrived in this world until the moment I leave it, I will always carry you in my heart.
—MANDY HARRISON

second
Trimester

Congratulations! You've made it to the second trimester of your pregnancy, a magical time. Morning sickness disappears, and energy and appetite re-emerge. You begin to feel your baby kick for the first time. Your belly is expanding, but you're not yet experiencing the discomfort and pains of the third trimester.

This also a great time to take pre-baby getaway and a birthing and infant cardiopulmonary resuscitation (CPR) class. Encourage loved ones who will be helping you care for your baby to take this class as well. Infant CPR classes may be offered at the hospital where you plan to give birth. The hospital may also offer tours of the maternity ward.

As your body continues to grow, you will need to find maternity clothing or stretchy clothing in larger sizes. Look for consignment sales and consider borrowing maternity clothes from other moms to save money since maternity clothes can be quite expensive when you consider your growing belly.

Did you know?

- Babies are born with 300 bones that eventually fuse together to make 206 bones by adulthood.

- After 28 weeks of pregnancy, you may be required by certain airlines to obtain a doctor's note stating that you are sufficiently healthy for air travel. Airlines completely restrict air travel after 36 weeks of pregnancy—32 weeks for women carrying twins.

- The word placenta is derived from the Greek term for "flat cake."

Baby is the size of a shrimp

measuring about 3 inches in length and weighing 0.75 ounce. Vocal cords are developing, and the eyes are making their way toward the front of the face. If baby is a girl, she now has a lifetime supply of eggs—between one and two million—in her ovaries.

You may be feeling like you need to pee all the time. That urge signals that your body is working hard to circulate nutrients and remove waste toxins. The activity puts you at a higher risk of developing bladder infections. Drinking cranberry juice and lots of water, and peeing when you feel the urge, can help prevent these infections.

For the second trimester, I'm most excited about

A mother is always the beginning.
She is how things begin.
—AMY TAN

The first items I bought or am planning to buy for you are

Memorable well wishes and baby gifts I've received so far:

Baby is the size of a lemon

measuring about 3.5 inches in length and weighing close to 1 ounce. Baby can now frown, squint, and grasp things. Your baby is also practicing inhaling and exhaling, which is essential to forming air sacs in the lungs. Sweat glands are working, and fingernails and toenails are starting to develop.

The pigmentation of your nipples may darken, and your areolas may enlarge. These changes are completely normal. You may already be producing colostrum, the antibody-rich fluid that feeds the baby before your milk comes in.

Since becoming pregnant, I most appreciate these things about my loved ones:

I'm planning to include loved ones in my pregnancy experience by

These folks have been by my side through my pregnancy journey:

Since learning I was pregnant, the nicest surprise I received from a loved one is

Maternity is a glorious thing, since all mankind has been conceived, born, and nourished of women. All human laws should encourage the multiplication of families.

—MARTIN LUTHER

Week 15

Baby is the size of an apple or pear

measuring around 4 inches in length and weighing nearly 2 ounces. Baby now fits in the palm of your hand. All four limbs, along with joints, are fully functional, so your baby can move like never before. The neck and mouth are newly defined and also moving. Even so, you may not feel much activity yet.

Because your lungs share space with your growing baby, they have less room to expand, making you feel easily winded. Your body is also routing more oxygen to support developing tissue. Blood flow to the uterus and kidneys is increasing, thanks to your body's naturally increasing blood volume and red blood cell count.

Many moms begin preparing for the arrival of their babies in earnest at this stage. But preparation should go beyond considering which color to paint the baby's nursery or other space. If you plan to return to work after the baby arrives, begin researching your employer's paid and unpaid leave policy, the Family and Medical Leave Act, your partner's eligibility for family leave from work, and daycare facilities in your area.

I think it'd be fun to have a girl because

I think it'd be fun to have a boy because

I'm planning to [find out your sex / be surprised] because

Names I'm currently considering:

The life of a mother is the life of a child: you are two blossoms on a single branch.
—KAREN MAEZEN MILLER

Baby is the size of an avocado

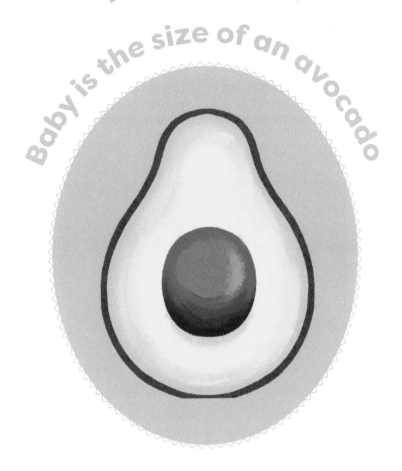

measuring about 4.5 inches in length and weighing 2.5 ounces. Baby's nose is fully formed, and the body begins growing faster than the head. Delicate bones in the eyebrows and ears are forming, and eyelashes and hair are beginning to sprout. Your baby can make a fist and suck on a thumb.

This week, your placenta weighs as much as your baby. By the time you give birth, however, the placenta will weigh between one and two pounds. The placenta plays many vital roles, aiding waste removal, digestion, and respiration, and protecting and preparing your body for milk creation through hormone production.

I've been calling you (nickname)

Loved ones have called you

Some features and qualities of mine I hope you have:

Sometimes the strength of motherhood is greater than natural laws.
—BARBARA KINGSOLVER

Some features and qualities of your mother/father I hope you have:

Some features and qualities of other family members I hope you have:

Baby is the size of a pomegranate

measuring about 5 inches in length and weighing about 6 ounces. Kidneys have matured, and reflex behavior should be kicking in. Fingers and toes are so well defined that baby now has unique fingerprints.

You may be able to really feel the baby as early as this week, but do not worry if you don't. Most moms won't feel first kicks until sometime between 20 and 22 weeks. This week is a good time to prepare for your baby's anatomy scan, which usually takes place when you are 18 to 20 weeks pregnant. Write down a list of questions for the doctor, along with any concerns or symptoms you may have. Remember, there are no dumb questions when it comes to your health or the health of your baby.

Pregnancy is known to trigger vivid dreams. Some of my most

memorable dreams have been

I [have / haven't] had dreams about certain foods that made me crave them.

My current food cravings:

My current food aversions:

Mama was my greatest teacher, a teacher of compassion, love and fearlessness. If love is sweet as a flower, then my mother is that sweet flower of love.
—STEVIE WONDER

Baby is the size of an artichoke

measuring 6 inches in length and weighing 8.5 ounces. Baby may be kicking, twisting, punching, and rolling. The eyes can move from side to side and are sensitive to light. Your baby is now also sensitive to loud noises and can hear your voice and heartbeat.

After a meal, your baby will receive nutrients from your food within a couple of hours. You know what also begins to happen after meals now? Heartburn. There are some easy steps you can take to avoid it. For one, avoid laying down for a couple of hours after eating. Breaking big meals up into several smaller ones and drinking lots of water between meals can also help.

I [am / am not] planning to have a baby shower.

Ways I've been connecting and communicating with you:

How I'm sleeping lately:

Birth is about making mothers—strong, competent, capable mothers who trust themselves and know their inner strength.
—BARBARA KATZ ROTHMAN

Week 19

Baby is the size of a mango

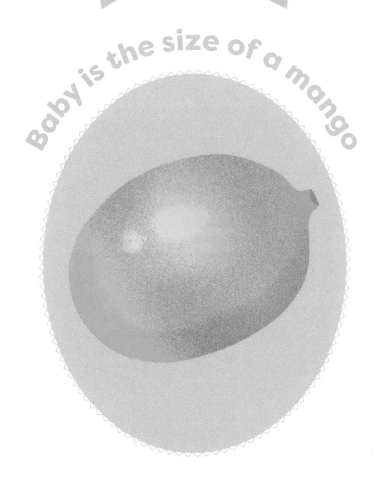

measuring 6 inches in length and weighing 8.5 ounces. The nerve cells that make up baby's five senses are now developing in the brain. This month baby will grow a whopping 2 inches in length. Their heart is now pumping 25 quarts of blood each day. By the time your baby is born, the heart will pump 300 quarts a day.

And congratulations, mama: You are officially halfway through your pregnancy! Before you know it, you will be welcoming a baby boy or girl into the world. Speaking of which, the second trimester ultrasound, also known as the anomaly scan, which usually takes place between weeks 18 and 20, can now confirm if you are having a boy or a girl. If you are having a boy, the penis and scrotum should be visible.

I've decided [to / not to] find out your sex before the birth.

How I feel about finding out your sex:

How family and loved ones are reacting:

How I'm feeling about the anomaly scan:

Baby is the size of a banana

measuring around 6.5 inches in length and weighing 10 ounces. Baby is likely becoming increasingly active inside your belly. At first, the kicks may feel like popping bubbles or fluttering butterflies. As your baby's body grows, you may feel like you are carrying a miniature professional soccer player.

If you want to trigger the baby to move and kick, drink an ice-cold glass of juice and then lie down. Together, your stillness, the sugar from the juice, and the coldness from the ice will have your baby performing!

Place your sonogram
photo here

How I'm feeling about the 20-week sonogram:

Seeing you more fully formed in the sonogram made me feel

Children in a family are like flowers in a bouquet: there's always one determined to face in an opposite direction from the way the arranger desires.
—MARCELENE COX

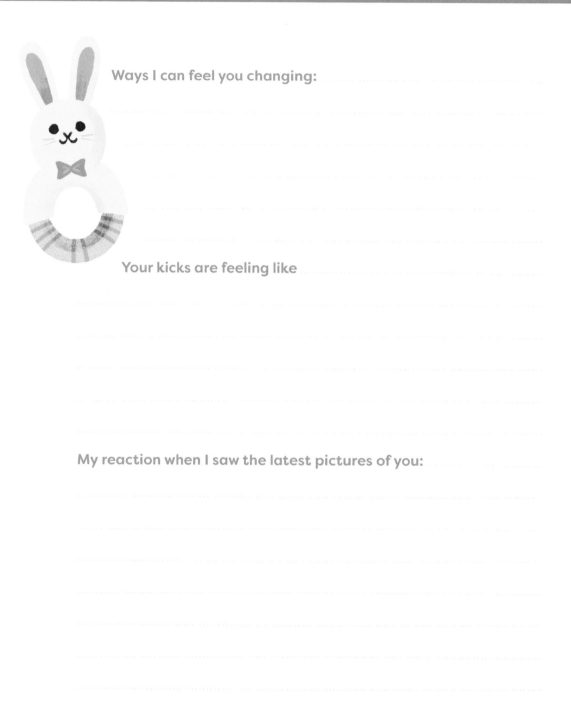

Ways I can feel you changing:

Your kicks are feeling like

My reaction when I saw the latest pictures of you:

Baby is the size of a carrot

measuring 10.5 inches in length and weighing about 13 ounces. (It may seem like a significant growth spurt, but after week 20, your doctor starts measuring baby from head to toe.) Baby's first teeth are developing in the gums, and the tongue is fully formed.

The hair on your baby's head may also be growing in and may be as long as an inch. A girl's uterus is fully formed, and her vagina, hymen, and labia are developing. A boy's testes have begun descending from the pelvis to the scrotum.

Your baby needs about 200 calories a day, so if your intake before pregnancy was 2,100 calories a day, you will want to increase it to 2,300 calories a day. Most weight will be gained after 20 weeks, so break out your maternity clothes if you haven't already. Don't worry about the extra weight. During pregnancy, it's normal for women to gain as much as 40 pounds, depending on their starting weight.

My approach to maternity wear:

My favorite pregnancy outfit:

I [am / am not] planning to do a maternity photo shoot.

How I'm feeling about my changing body:

Making the decision to have a child—it is momentous. It is to decide forever to have your heart go walking around outside your body.
—ELIZABETH STONE

Baby is the size of a grapefruit

measuring 11 inches in length and weighing 15 ounces. Baby is sleeping between 12 and 16 hours each day, the same number of hours as a newborn. Baby's brain is growing rapidly, and hearing has gained acuity. Loud music or a dog barking can now wake your baby from sleep.

On the flip side, your baby may respond positively to soothing music and your voice. Familiar sounds will help the baby transition from your womb to the world.

The bigger your baby grows, the more you will feel it. Rhythmic pops coming from your belly every two to four seconds and lasting as long as a half hour are hiccups.

Ways family and loved ones are engaging with you in my belly:

Life is always a rich and steady time when you are waiting for something to happen or to hatch.
—E. B. WHITE

Things that seem to calm you down when you're active:

I notice you moving when (activities or times of day)

Baby is the size of a zucchini

measuring about 11.5 inches and weighing 1 full pound. Baby's eyes are developed, but the iris still has no color. Baby's body is also becoming more proportionate, and they can now stroke his or her own face.

As your belly stretches, you may feel quite itchy. There are many fantastic creams and oils to soothe the skin as it grows. Your uterus is now the size of a soccer ball, and you likely feel your baby's movement, but it may take a few more weeks for others to feel it.

How you're feeling in my belly:

How I'm feeling about your arrival:

Things I'm doing to prepare for your arrival:

Things I want to do before you come:

The moment a child is born, the mother is also born.
She never existed before. The woman existed, but the
mother, never. A mother is something absolutely new.

—OSHO

Baby is the size of an ear of corn

measuring almost 12 inches in length and weighing 1.3 pounds. Baby's muscles and nervous system are developing, and all major organs, except for the lungs, are fully functional. New blood vessels in the lungs oxygenate your baby's blood. With fully formed facial features, your baby now looks much as he or she will look at birth.

By now, you should be gaining approximately one pound per week. As your body takes on extra weight and fluid, you may also notice that your feet and ankles are beginning to swell. Resting and elevating your legs will alleviate the swelling.

So far, the biggest surprise during this pregnancy has been

Things I wish people had told me about pregnancy:

My mom smiles at me. Her smile kind of hugged me.

—R. J. PALACIO

Advice I would give a newly expecting mom:

What I want to remember from this pregnancy so far:

Baby is the size of a head of lettuce

measuring about 13 inches in length and weighing 1.5 pounds. Baby's hair color is defined, and the skin is becoming opaque as the body gains much-needed fat. The cells that create conscious thought are now developing in the brain.

It's never too early to start doing some pelvic exercises. Strengthening your pelvic floor muscles with Kegel exercises will help treat urine incontinence and improve sexual function (especially after the baby is born). You can do Kegel exercises anytime and anywhere, without anyone suspecting a thing.

Write a love letter to your baby.

A strong intention, a relaxed body and an open mind are the main ingredients for an active birth.

—JANET BALASKAS

Now write a love letter to your 18-year-old child.

My favorite family memories:

65

Baby is the size of a rutabaga

measuring 14 inches in length and 1.7 pounds. The air sacs in baby's lungs develop and inflate, allowing baby to take tiny breaths of amniotic fluid. Until birth, all of your baby's oxygen comes from you through the umbilical cord and placenta. By now, the nostrils have started to prepare them to breathe air.

Your third trimester woes may have begun by now. You may experience pain under the ribs as your large and small intestines shove your abdomen. You may also notice that your equilibrium is off, causing you to be more prone to tripping, so take extra caution and avoid high heels.

How I'm feeling different from previous weeks:

What I miss:

Giving birth should be your greatest achievement, not your greatest fear.

—JANE WEIDEMAN

What I'm looking forward to:

Ways my movements have changed:

Pregnancy brain [has / has not] affected me so far.

Baby is the size of a head of cauliflower

measuring about 14.5 inches in length and weighing almost two pounds. The lungs are now capable of inhaling and exhaling air, and brain activity has officially begun.

In this fast-growth phase, you may increase your calorie intake by 300 calories a day, consuming approximately 2,400 total calories on a daily basis. And thanks to the baby's rapid growth and movement, others should now be able to feel the baby kick.

Names I'm considering and their meanings:

Pregnancy is getting company inside one's skin.
—MAGGIE SCARF

Your last name will be:

It means:

Reactions of others when theyve noticed you moving:

third Trimester

Congratulations on making it to the final stretch! What happens during the third trimester makes the idea of bringing a child into this world very real.

You are now housing an active little kicker, people are noticing your growing belly, and you're nesting in preparation for your baby's arrival. From birthing classes to babyproofing, from decorating the nursery or other space in your home to registering for your baby shower, you may feel like you have many tasks—but little energy to do them all. Don't stress the little details. What needs to get done will get done, and what doesn't get done probably isn't all that important.

Writing things down can help you get organized and overcome anxiety. At the end of this section, there is a place to describe your birth plan (see page 130). Writing down your birth plan may help ease some angst by allowing you to visualize how you hope everything will play out.

Try to remain flexible and keep an open mind when it comes to your birth plan. Giving birth is a major life event, and like many major life events, it can come with surprises and unexpected detours. Planning for a baby is a lot like planning for a wedding. If the big day brings rain, the couple has no choice but to adapt to the weather. That's how you should approach your baby's birth. Make your plans, but be ready to adapt, understanding that a safe delivery and healthy baby are what matter most.

Week 28

Baby is the size of an eggplant

measuring 15 inches in length and 2.3 pounds. Baby is now aware of external light. The brain is tripling in weight, and your baby may be able to dream. The skin begins looking less wrinkly as fat grows under it.

Your body may feel achier than it has in the past. A heating pad can alleviate sciatica pain, which results from your baby's repositioning to prepare for birth. Other symptoms, like bloating and gas, may emerge or increase. Remember, your organs have less room as your belly grows, so there is bound to be some discomfort.

If you're having a baby shower, you may be registering at your favorite stores for baby essentials. If you're not having a baby shower, you may be conducting product research and buying everything from baby furniture to newborn clothing. While your body is busy growing a human, your physical space is beginning to truly reflect the new addition to your family.

Major items I have in place for your arrival:

Things I still need/plan to get:

New symptoms I'm noticing:

You [don't seem to / seem to] respond to external light.

Life is a gift given in trust . . . like a child.
—ANNE MORROW LINDBERGH

Week 29

Baby is the size of an acorn squash

measuring 15.3 inches in length and weighing 2.7 pounds. The eyelids have unfused and can open partially. By week 29, baby's sense of touch and other senses are developing.

A great way to keep track of how often your baby moves is to do "kick counts" during the same one- to two-hour period each day. You should be able to track 10 fetal movements in less than two hours. Record the number of kicks, and if something seems off, report it to your obstetrician.

Many local police and fire stations offer free car seat installation. If you are new to using a car seat, take advantage of this popular service.

Where I plan to give birth:

Ways I've prepared for birth:

When I go into labor, I plan to call:

The most important things in life aren't things.
—ANTHONY J. D'ANGELO

Week 30

Baby is the size of a large cabbage

measuring 15 and 0.7 inches in length and weighing almost 3 pounds. Baby is now peeing a pint of urine each day. The eye-lids can fully open and close, and your baby is already hard at work perfecting the side eye and eye rolls you'll be seeing for decades to come.

Your baby's rapid growth puts a lot of pressure on your bladder, which explains your frequent urges to use the bathroom. At the same time, you are likely to experience an increase in water retention, leading to swelling in your face, feet, ankles, and hands. Remove any rings on your fingers to prevent them from becoming stuck. You can put them on a chain and wear them as a necklace until the swelling goes down.

What will be/is in my hospital bag:

How I'm feeling about giving birth:

Your first outfit will be:

I can be covered in spit-up on a conference call while I'm pumping and that's OK, because this is my perfect. It may not be somebody else's, but this is mine.
—KERRY WASHINGTON

Baby is the size of a coconut

measuring 16 inches in length and weighing 3.3 pounds. As the womb becomes increasingly snug, baby's legs will fold next to the chest.

At this stage of your pregnancy, fluctuating hormones, stress, and dehydration may cause headaches. Make sure to drink lots of water. Doing so will also help combat stretch marks.

As a child, my favorite books were:

My favorite games to play were:

My favorite TV or film characters were:

Ways I hope your childhood will be similar to mine:

Ways I hope your childhood will be different from mine:

There is a secret in our culture, and it's not that birth is painful. It's that women are strong.
—LAURA STAVOE HARM

Week 32

Baby is the size of a celery stalk

measuring more than 16.5 inches in length and weighing 3.5 pounds. Baby can see, hear, taste, and touch but cannot smell until able to breathe air.

At this stage, you may begin experiencing Braxton-Hicks contractions. They are essentially "practice" contractions, which help prepare you for labor. Switching positions can often ease these types of contractions, which may feel like cramping and tightening around the belly and lower back pain. Although Braxton-Hicks contractions will increase as you near your due date, they should still only be occasional. If you notice your contractions begin to develop a pattern and feel increasingly stronger, or you notice that you can no longer walk or talk during a contraction, you should contact your obstetrician immediately or head to the hospital, because these are signs of active labor.

I [have / haven't] had Braxton-Hicks contractions.

What I know/how I feel about them:

My belly [has / hasn't] dropped yet in preparation for birth.

How your movements are changing as you grow:

Becoming a mother has opened up my whole life and given me a whole new purpose. I feel like a star at home only because she loves me so much. I mean, it's a red carpet every day. It's wonderful!
                                                                    —VIOLA DAVIS

Week 33

Baby is the size of a large butternut squash

measuring nearly 17 inches in length and weighing close to 4 pounds. As baby gains one-third of his or her total weight and the volume of amniotic fluid reaches its peak, you may feel like your belly is suddenly getting much bigger.

Ossification of your baby's skeleton is occurring at a rapid pace during the last 12 weeks of pregnancy. During this time, make sure your calcium intake is especially high to promote healthy bone development in your baby.

The best advice my parents gave me:

Birth is the epicenter of women's power.
—ANI DIFRANCO

What I learned from my parents that I hope to pass on to you:

The role I hope my parents and family will play in your life:

Baby is the size of a cantaloupe

measuring 17.5 inches in length and weighing 4.5 pounds. The first color that baby will see is the pinkish red inside of your womb. Your baby is now busy mastering a skill that may carry over after birth—thumb or finger sucking.

While the rest of your baby is developing, the bones in your baby's skull remain unfused, so that they can overlap to allow the head to pass through the birth canal without harm.

You may start to see little feet and hands press against your belly as your baby moves. Many women experience blurry vision and dry eyes around this time. Although those symptoms are temporary, be sure to mention them to your obstetrician, because they sometimes point to preeclampsia. Your back may continue to hurt and your digestive system may feel sluggish, but remember that the finish line is just around the corner.

I think you'll have _____ (color) eyes because _____

I think you'll have _____ (color) hair because _____

I [have / haven't] seen your hands or feet pressing against my belly.

My belly feels

In giving birth to our babies, we may find that we give birth to new possibilities within ourselves.
—MYLA AND JON KABAT-ZINN

Week 35

Baby is the size of a pineapple

measuring 1.5 feet in length and weighing 5 pounds. Baby's kidneys and liver can now process waste. With each day and week that passes, the likelihood that your baby will be born without complications improves greatly. So, continue to take it easy and stay well hydrated.

Heartburn may peak with increased pressure on your stomach and intestines. Half of all pregnant women will experience heartburn in the second and third trimesters. Heartburn feels like a burning sensation in the throat and is caused by food particles coming back up from the stomach, causing reflux. Talk to your doctor before taking over-the-counter antacids. A good at-home remedy is yogurt.

The most trying symptom of this pregnancy has been

The ways I've coped with fatigue during this pregnancy have been

The most unexpected symptom I've experienced so far has been

Birthing is the most profound initiation to spirituality a woman can have.

— ROBIN LIM

Baby is the size of a head of romaine

measuring 18.5 inches in length and weighing 5.5 pounds. Baby's fingernails and toenails have now fully grown in. Your baby's hearing is also super sensitive during this time, so much so that he or she can differentiate voices.

Now let's talk about "baby brain." Do you feel extra clumsy or forgetful? Do you feel stressed and anxious? Those feelings are perfectly normal, given the immense demands on your body. The good news is that they are temporary. The bad news is that years from now, "baby brain" will be replaced with "mom brain."

Since I've been pregnant, strangers have treated me

To be pregnant is to be vitally alive, thoroughly woman, and distressingly inhabited. Soul and spirit are stretched—along with body—making pregnancy a time of transition, growth, and profound beginnings.
— ANNE CHRISTIAN BUCHANAN

How I've dealt with rude comments or looks because of my belly:

Unexpected kind acts and compliments I've been given while pregnant:

How I feel about all the attention pregnant women receive:

Baby is the size of a winter melon

measuring 19 inches in length and weighing 6 pounds. Baby's movement is increasingly restricted due to limited space in your womb, which places a lot of pressure on your bladder and digestive system. The baby drops into your pelvis, which should relieve pressure on your lungs, making it easier for you to breathe.

Some pregnant moms experience "leaky boob" before the baby arrives, which is totally normal. The yellowish fluid, called colostrum, is also nicknamed "liquid gold" because it is rich in nutrients that support immunity, growth, and tissue repair. Colostrum is the nourishment that the baby receives before mother's milk comes in.

When I plan to/started to babyproof our home:

[Motherhood] *is full of complex emotions of joy, exhaustion, love, and worry, all mixed together. Your fundamental identity changes overnight.*
—KATE MIDDLETON

How I'm spending my days:

How my daily/work schedule has changed:

My plans for the coming months:

Week 38

Baby is the size of a stalk of rhubarb

measuring around 19.5 inches and weighing 6.5 pounds. The air sacs in baby's lungs will now open. The light fuzz that covered your baby for warmth is now falling away to prepare for life outside your womb. Baby's nervous system and brain are being fine-tuned in preparation for a world of stimuli.

Congratulations! Your pregnancy is now considered full term! During this week's prenatal checkup, your obstetrician will likely check your cervix, which is likely 2.5 to 5 centimeters dilated. Your cervix will need to dilate to 10 centimeters for your baby to pass through it. The umbilical cord is transmitting about 300 quarts of fluid from the placenta to the baby during these last weeks of pregnancy. Your connective tissue is also loosening in preparation for your big day, possibly resulting in a waddle-like walk.

What I've loved most about the third trimester:

No one's really doing it perfectly. I think you love your kids with your whole heart, and you do the best you possibly can.
—REESE WITHERSPOON

What I've loathed most about the third trimester:

How my cravings have changed since the first and second trimesters:

How I would describe my overall pregnancy experience:

Baby is the size of a pumpkin

measuring 20 inches in length and weighing 7 pounds. Baby is now ready to arrive! All systems are a go. The brain, however, continues to grow. Baby's skin has changed to a whitish hue due to a layer of fat that now rests over the blood vessels.

Your Braxton-Hicks contractions are probably peaking right about now. However, the real contractions can start at any time, so keep your phone fully charged and place your hospital bag by the front door. Driving to the hospital in active labor is not safe, so make sure that your loved ones are on call during this time.

Intense pressure in the uterus lasting up to 50 seconds and then releasing means it may be time to get to the hospital. This pressure can feel like painful menstrual cramps and lower back pain. Start timing the number of minutes between each contraction and its duration. If contractions are four minutes apart, last at least one minute each, and continue for at least an hour, get to the hospital.

When I started experiencing Braxton-Hicks contractions:

In pregnancy, there are two bodies, one inside the other. Two people live under one skin. When so much of life is dedicated to maintaining our integrity as distinct beings, this bodily tandem is an uncanny fact.

—JOAN RAPHAEL-LEFF

Changes in my body:

Early labor signs I've had:

How I'm feeling about the birth:

Week 40

Baby is the size of a watermelon

measuring 20.5 inches in length and weighing about 7.5 pounds. By now, most of baby's vernix (the creamy protective substance covering the body) is gone. If you're at the tail end of week 40 and your baby is still nestled in your womb, don't worry. Many pregnancies go beyond 40 weeks.

In the days leading up to labor, your baby's head may exert pressure on your hips and bladder, leading to pain in your pelvis. Leg cramps are also common. Your water may break before or after you go into labor. Pay attention to how your contractions feel.

After birth, your body may look like it did when you were five months pregnant. Allow yourself some grace to heal and rest. You just grew and will have given birth to a human life. Try not to stress over losing your baby weight. Instead, savor the precious cuddling and bonding sessions between you and your baby.

How this pregnancy experience has differed from what I expected:

The biggest surprises from this pregnancy:

Advice I would give someone just finding out she is pregnant for this first time:

Once you bring life into this world, you must protect it. We must protect it by changing the world.
                              —ELIE WIESEL

How I'm feeling:

my *Birth Plan*

My name:

Partner's name:

Due date/induction date:

My birth team:

Hospital/birthing center name:

I plan to have a [vaginal / C-section / water birth / VBAC]

delivery.

Notes about me/baby:

Who I'd like present for labor and birth:

Labor atmosphere and preferences: ....

....

....

Laboring positions I'd like to try: ....

....

....

Techniques/reminders for me during labor: ....

....

....

Plans for pain management: ....

....

....

After-birth preferences: ....

....

....

Plans for visiting with family and friends following delivery:

....

....

Other notes: ....

....

....

129

Birth

Place photo here

(name of baby)

was born at

on

(time of birth)   (date of birth)

weighing

(pounds)   (ounces)

measuring   long

(inches)

with

eyes

(color)

and

hair

(color)

at

(place of birth)

I went into labor on .... (day) at ....
(time).

Where I was when I knew I had gone into active

labor: ....

My water [did / did not] break spontaneously.

.... (name) drove me to the hospital/birthing center.

Who was in the room when I delivered you: ....

....

....

....

Labor lasted (length of time): ....

Memorable moments from labor: ....

....

....

....

Who helped deliver you:

Who cut your umbilical cord:

What happened immediately after delivery:

Memorable moments from delivery:

When I first saw you, I

We stayed at the hospital for _____ (number) days.

What we did when we first came home:

NEWBORN FOOTPRINTS

(left foot)

(right foot)

baby's
First 12 Months

1 Month

Date:

Weight:

Length/Height:

Your sleep schedule:

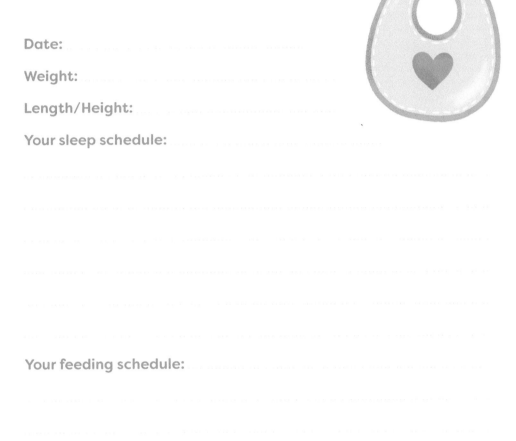

Your feeding schedule:

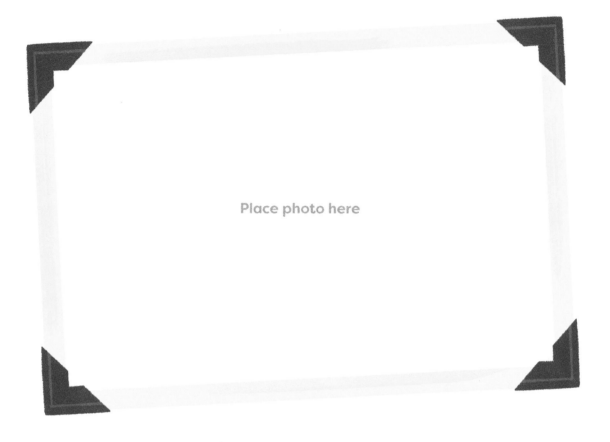

Place photo here

Milestones you've met:

> *Giving birth and being born brings us into the essence*
> *of creation, where the human spirit is courageous and*
> *bold, and the body a miracle of wisdom.*
>
> —HARRIETTE HARTIGAN

Places you've visited:

People you've met:

New discoveries and achievements:

Memorable moments:

2 Months

Date:

Weight:

Length/Height:

Your sleep schedule:

Your feeding schedule:

No influence is so powerful as that of the mother.
—SARAH JOSEPHA HALE

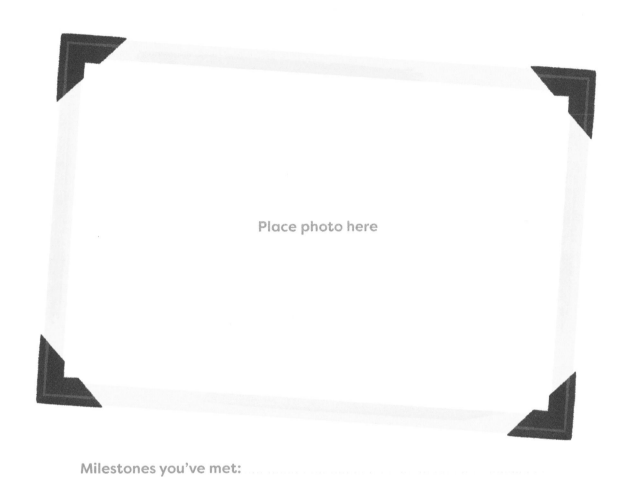

Place photo here

Milestones you've met:

Places you've visited:

People you've met:

New discoveries and achievements:

Memorable moments:

3 Months

Date:

Weight:

Length/Height:

Your sleep schedule:

Your feeding schedule:

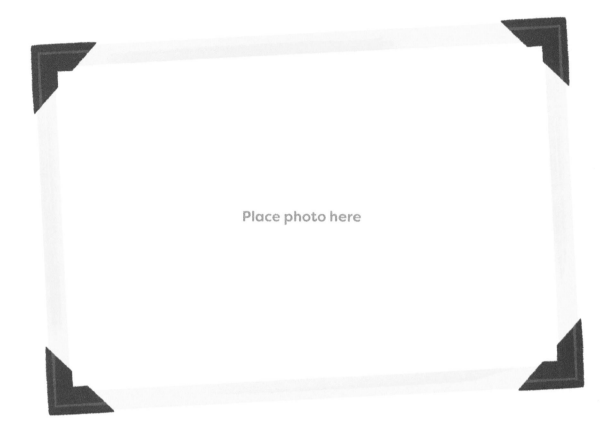

Place photo here

Milestones you've met:

[Motherhood] is the biggest gamble in the world. It is the glorious life force. It's huge and scary—it's an act of infinite optimism.
—GILDA RADNER

Places you've visited:

People you've met:

New discoveries and achievements:

Memorable moments:

4 Months

Date:

Weight:

Length/Height:

Your sleep schedule:

Your feeding schedule:

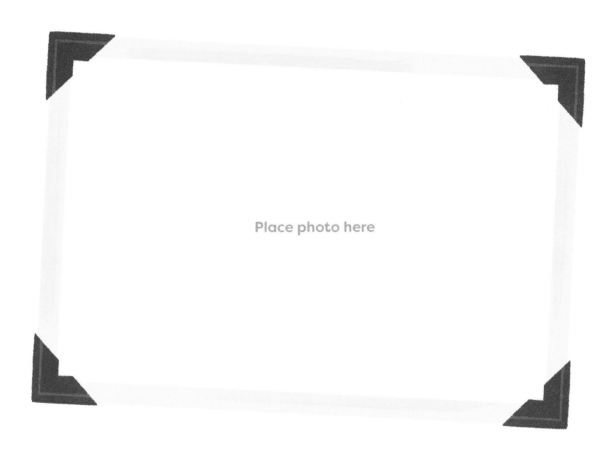

Place photo here

Milestones you've met:

> We worry about what a child will
> become tomorrow, yet we forget that
> [they are] *someone today.*
> —STACIA TAUSCHER

Places you've visited:

People you've met:

New discoveries and achievements:

Memorable moments:

5
Months

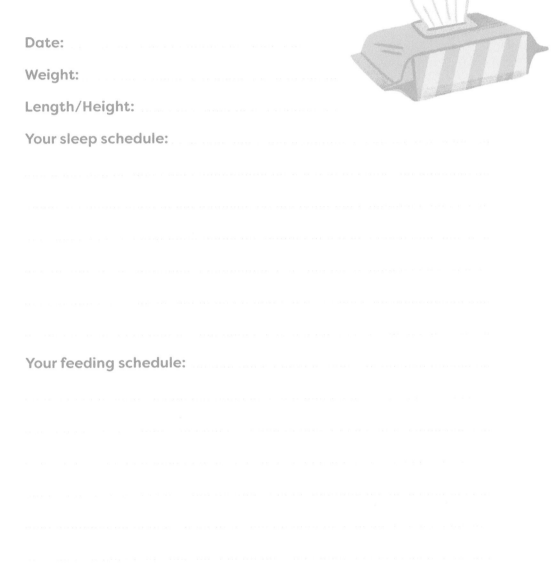

Date:

Weight:

Length/Height:

Your sleep schedule:

Your feeding schedule:

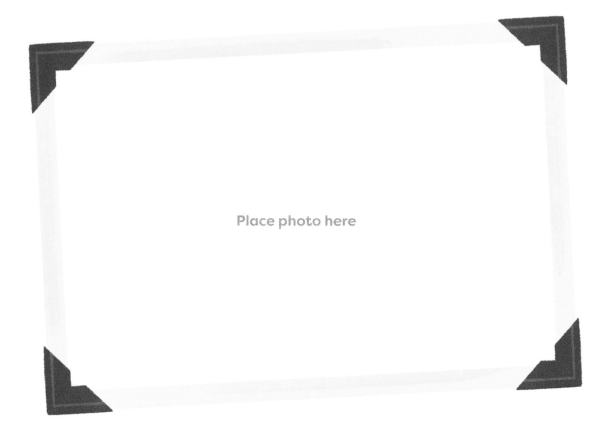

Place photo here

Milestones you've met:

A mother continues to labor long after the baby is born.

—LISA-JO BAKER

Places you've visited:

People you've met:

New discoveries and achievements:

Memorable moments:

6 Months

Date:

Weight:

Length/Height:

Your sleep schedule:

Your feeding schedule:

Your favorite and new foods:

There's no way to be a perfect mother and a million ways to be a good one.
—JILL CHURCHILL

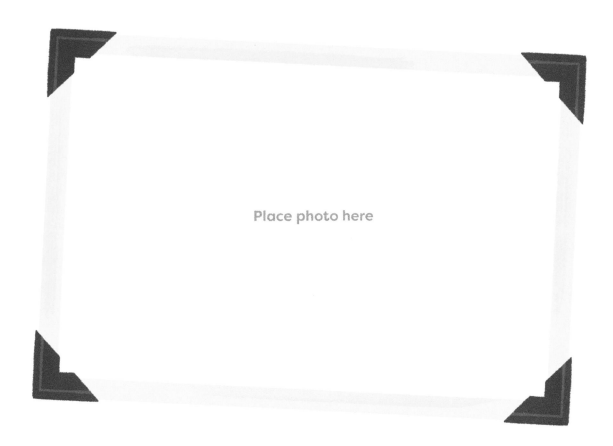

Place photo here

Milestones you've met:

Places you've visited:

People you've met:

New discoveries and achievements:

Memorable moments:

7 Months

Date:

Weight:

Length/Height:

Your daily rhythm:

Your favorite and new foods:

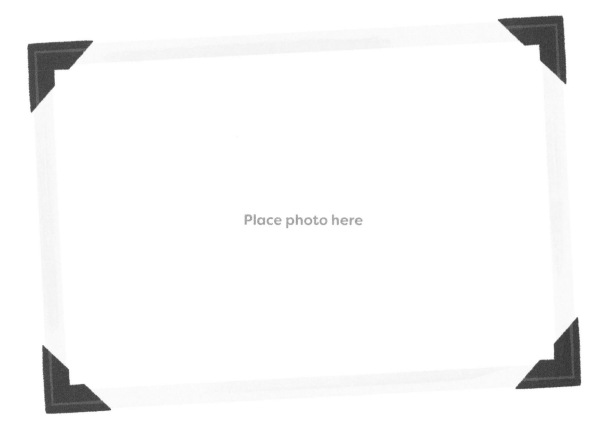

Place photo here

Milestones you've met:

Being a mom has made me so tired.
And so happy.

—TINA FEY

Places you've visited:

People you've met:

New discoveries and achievements:

Memorable moments:

8 Months

Date:

Weight:

Length/Height:

Your daily rhythm:

Your favorite and new foods:

Children are not only innocent and curious, but also optimistic and joyful and essentially happy. They are, in short, everything adults wish they could be.

—CAROLYN HAYWOOD

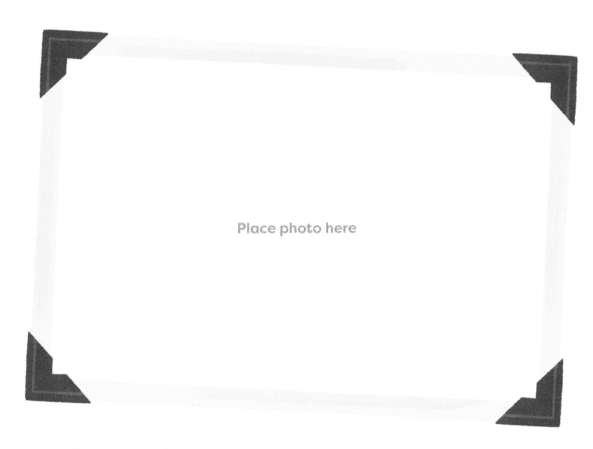

Place photo here

Milestones you've met:

Places you've visited:

People you've met:

New discoveries and achievements:

Memorable moments:

9 Months

Date:

Weight:

Length/Height:

Your daily rhythm:

Your favorite and new foods:

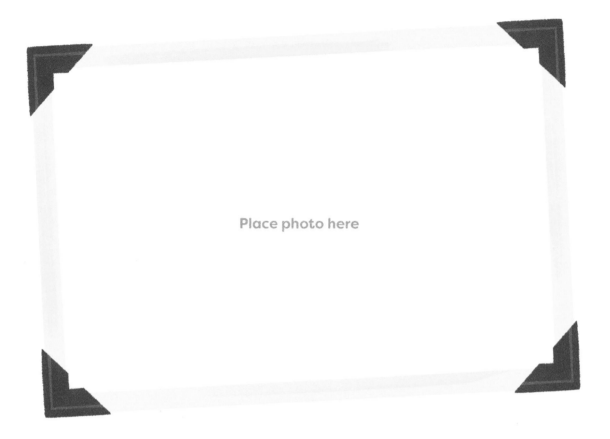

Place photo here

Milestones you've met:

Children are likely to live up to what you believe of them.
—LADY BIRD JOHNSON

Places you've visited:

People you've met:

New discoveries and achievements:

Memorable moments:

10 Months

Date:

Weight:

Length/Height:

Your daily rhythm:

Your favorite and new foods:

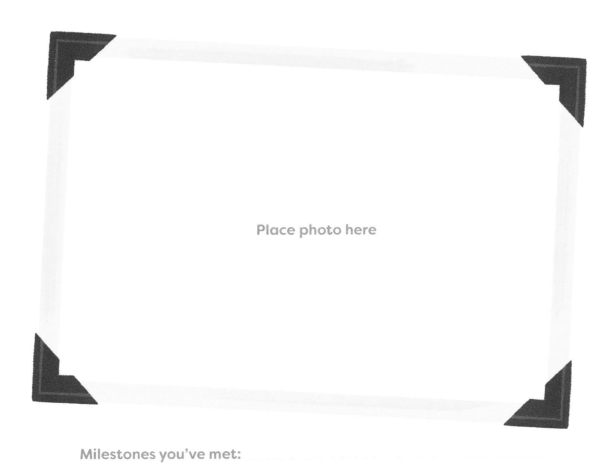

Place photo here

Milestones you've met:

> *The biggest surprise, which is also the best, is that I didn't know I would love motherhood as much as I do.*
> —DEBORAH NORVILLE

Places you've visited:

People you've met:

New discoveries and achievements:

Memorable moments:

11 Months

Date:

Weight:

Length/Height:

Your daily rhythm:

Your favorite and new foods:

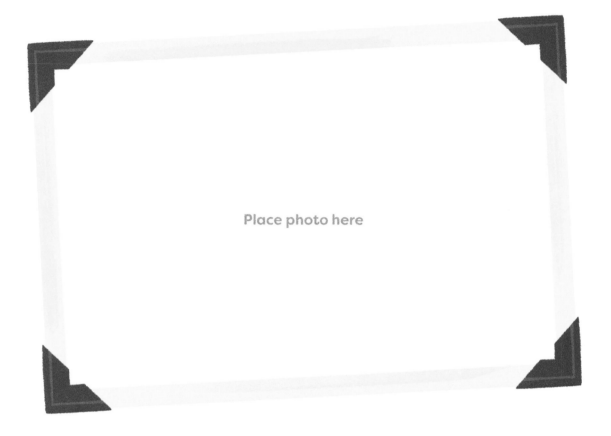

Place photo here

Milestones you've met:

Having kids—the responsibility of rearing good, kind, ethical, responsible human beings—is the biggest job anyone can embark on.

—MARIA SHRIVER

Places you've visited:

People you've met:

New discoveries and achievements:

Memorable moments:

12 Months

Date:

Weight:

Length/Height:

Your daily rhythm:

Your favorite and new foods:

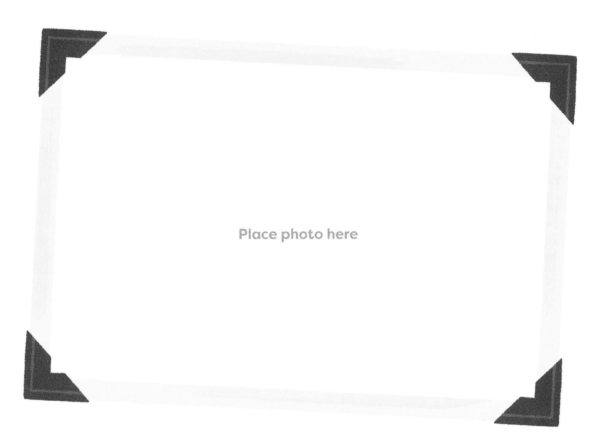

Place photo here

Milestones you've met:

> *Hugs can do great amounts of good, especially for children.*
> —DIANA, PRINCESS OF WALES

Places you've visited:

People you've met:

New discoveries and achievements:

Memorable moments:

1-YEAR FOOTPRINTS

(left foot)

(right foot)

firsts and *Favorites*

First bath:

First time rolling over:

First time smiling:

First time laughing:

First time sitting up:

First time sleeping through the night:

First time trying solids:

First food:

First tooth came in:

First time waving:

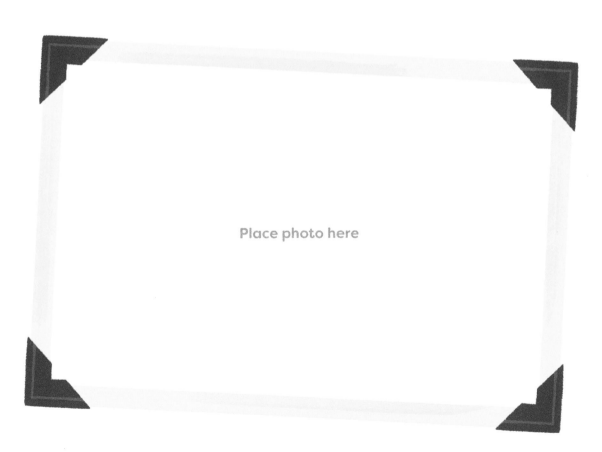

Place photo here

First time clapping:

First time babbling:

First friend:

First time crawling:

First time cruising:

First time standing:

First steps:

First words:

First trip: _____

_____

First haircut: _____

_____

_____

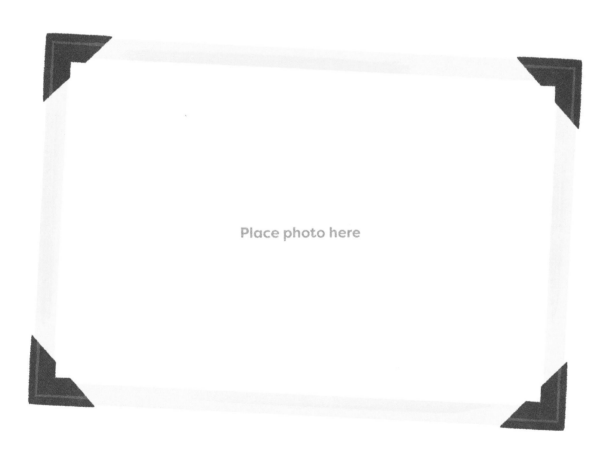

Place photo here

First holiday:

Favorite song:

Favorite toy:

Favorite book:

Favorite stuffed animal:

Favorite game:

Favorite food:

Favorite activity:

Favorite friend:

Least favorite things:

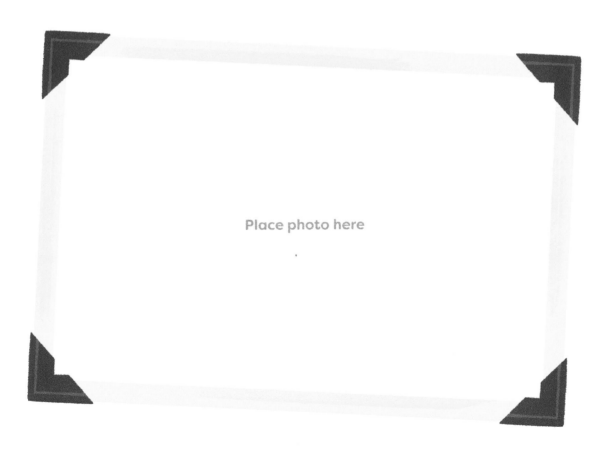

Place photo here

growth *Chart*

Month One

Height: .... Weight: ....

Month Two

Height: .... Weight: ....

Month Three

Height: .... Weight: ....

Month Four

Height: .... Weight: ....

Month Five

Height: .... Weight: ....

Month Six

Height: .... Weight: ....

Month Seven

Height: .... Weight: ....

Month Eight

Height: .... Weight: ....

Month Nine

Height: .... Weight: ....

Month Ten

Height: .... Weight: ....

Month Eleven

Height: .... Weight: ....

Month Twelve

Height: .... Weight: ....

baby's
First Birthday

Place photo here

Your first birthday party was on .... (date)

at .... (location).

Theme and decorations:

Who was there:

What we ate:

Highlights of the day:

Memorable things you've done:

Memorable gifts:

ABOUT THE AUTHOR

Lucy Riles is the founder of Life of Mom, mother to four children and two dogs, and wife to Tom Riles, founder of Life of Dad. In addition to her role as "human creator," Lucy is also a content creator, writer, performer, and storyteller.

The youngest of 12 children, Lucy grew up on the South Side of Chicago and was raised by two amazing parents, Barbara and Jim Bansley. After graduating from Ball State University, Lucy moved to Los Angeles, 2,000 miles away from "her village," to pursue a career in entertainment.

Lucy's entrance into motherhood was both terrifying and isolating. At 20 weeks pregnant, her firstborn was diagnosed with a serious heart condition requiring life-saving open-heart surgery. She turned to social media searching for love and support.

In 2016, Lucy founded a "virtual village" for moms worldwide called Life of Mom. She has substantially grown this judgment-free platform for moms by sharing her own authentic journey through motherhood.

Lucy's goal is and has always been to support and celebrate moms. Life of Mom is here to remind you that you are not alone on this wild ride called motherhood.

Lucy is thrilled to report that she has found her village within the incredible Life of Mom community.

CPSIA information can be obtained
at www.ICGtesting.com
Printed in the USA
BVHW091313300919
559795BV00003B/3/P